MIND ROOMS GUIDE

Handbook to Bypass "Overwhelm," Make More Time,
& Shape Your Work Flow with Meaning & Delight

TRACKING WONDER

TABLE OF CONTENTS

MIND ROOMS GUIDE: Handbook to Bypass "Overwhelm," Make More Time, &
Shape Your Work Flow with Meaning & Delight
by Jeffrey Davis

Copyright © 2015 by Jeffrey Davis & Tracking Wonder

Miro Press
Hudson Valley of New York

ISBN-10: 0-9908319-2-2
ISBN-13: 978-0-9908319-2-1

156 Upper Whitfield Rd. Accord. NY 12404
845.679.9441 www.trackingwonder.com

My first baby girl's birth was a wake-up call to my relationship to time and creativity. I burned with so many projects to advance. In one year, I was developing a book, launching teaching programs, designing live events, and meeting responsibilities to speak and present and write while also building a business and, yes, being an attentive husband, partner, and papa.

But I refused to give into the stories of overwhelm I had heard from entrepreneur parents and creative parents. Yes, I experienced and still experience overwhelm in moments, but I was not going to live in overwhelm for weeks, months, years.

So, I started experimenting with how to shape time. Every planner and time management system I tried failed to understand how to motivate me – which is through meaning, purpose, and creativity.

That's when I came up with the Mind Rooms Method and then the Mind Rooms Guide.

It's small wonder why the Mind Rooms Guide has become such a hit with professionals and creatives.

Most Americans, according to a recent study, consider themselves creative and view creativity as important. But very few of them feel they're meeting their creative potential. Almost all Americans attributed this to insufficient time or lack of money to gain time. My clients and the audiences I had spoken to expressed similar frustrations. Their desires and ambitions did not line up with their perceived daily and weekly schedules or with their perceived priorities and visions.

Since we released the Mind Rooms Guide in 2012, executives, teachers, artists, consultants, coaches, health and wellness practitioners, parents, and more have shared with us their radically new relationship to time.

Two things have led to this expanded print edition of The Mind Rooms Guide.

One, I am obsessed with the nature of time & how to shape it. Over the past five years, I have published many pieces and reflections on the subject for the blog at TrackingWonder.com, for PsychologyToday.com, and for TheCreativityPost.com.

Two, many people in our international community have asked for a paper copy both for themselves and to buy as gifts for time-challenged friends, colleagues, team members, and loved ones.
Hence,

The updated Mind Rooms Guide - Paper Edition

With bonus essays, riffs, and tips on the art & science of shaping time

I hope this new Mind Rooms Guide inspires in you a renewed relationship to time, to your daily flow, and to what matters most for you to create in this one astonishing life.

It's possible. So much is.

Send me a note and a pic of your Mind Rooms. Maybe we will include it in our updated Mind Rooms Gallery.

Thanks for running with me,

Founder and Chief Tracker, Tracking Wonder Consultancy

THE HUT OF QUESTIONS

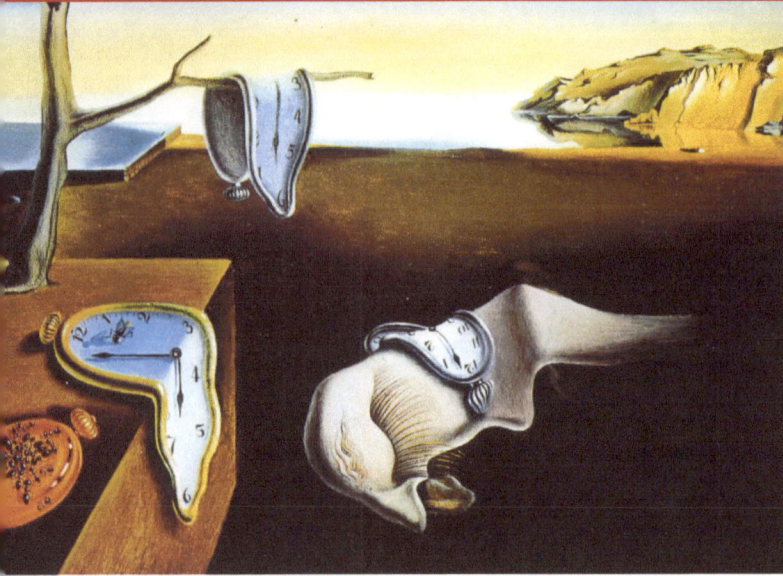

"[G]ood feelings such as affection, pride at a promotion, and enthusiasm for a new project are the carrots on the stick that keep you moving smartly along life's up-and-down road."

– WINIFRED GALLAGHER,
RAPT: Attention and the Focused Life
(Penguin Press, 2009)

Organization can dog the best of creatives. Many of my clients are authors, designers, corporate execs, and entrepreneurs who juggle multiple projects and obligations. I keep at least five projects in the air at any given time, each of which requires at least a few dozen tasks to complete.

I give clients and teams colored pencils and paper and ask them to sketch their individual relationship to time. What does it currently look like? Feel like? What images, objects, animals represent the relationship?

9 times out of 10, the relationship is burdensome and stressful. Few if any of them concur with Thoreau who writes, "Time is but the stream I go a-fishin' in."

> So how do we stay on top of those projects without driving ourselves daft and our intimate partners away?

> How can a small amount of time invested in flexible creative organization end up *making* time?

REFRAME: Creating *with* Chaos & Order

When it comes to time, several creatives fall sway to the whims of Eris, the Greek goddess of chaos. Eris likes to mix things up and keep us guessing. She thrives on surprise and novelty. Eris is essential for true wonder-tracking, deep problem-solving, and flat out being humble enough to know we're not in control of everything.

The Chaotic Creative knows Eris well.

The problem: Too much surrender to Eris after 10, 20 years as an adult, and the Chaotic Creatives I know and work with often feel frustrated with their lack of optimal productivity, depressed, and out of control.

Daily unexpected changes throw them easily off-track. They get lost in creative obsession. They forget what they want to do and what obligations they need to fulfill by certain time lines. They're full of inspired ideas but often lack a way to execute and follow through with those ideas.

And they run from anything smacking of "time management" because of the other extreme: The Rigid Creative. As the tag implies, every task has its place and time. There are morning routines and noon routines and evening routines. The RC tends to be highly productive and prolific. The downside? A hyper get-things-done disposition can short-circuit true inspiration and the depth of thought required to create work that really lasts and matters.

There is a third way, a Tracking Wonder way.

My experience as a writer and as a consultant who has worked with, studied, and interviewed numerous creatives, scientists, scholars, therapists, teachers, and others shows this:

Once we reach our middle years, over the long-term our best self

« thrives in a flexible structure
« thrives in a climate of delight & joy
« thrives with artful attention & intention
« feels deeply gratified upon completing project phases

THE RESEARCH OF FLOW

Creative organization can be a flexible, enjoyable way to shape attention, physical space, and actions. When we shape these three things — attention, space, and actions — we increase the likelihood that we can get in the flow state that psychologist Mihaly Cskiszentmihalyi describes.

For over 20 years, Cskiszentmihalyi has studied people who like to do things that they enjoy but are not rewarded for with money or fame. He has studied athletes, artists, religious mystics, scientists, chess players, rock climbers, and ordinary working people.

What keeps these creatives jazzed about what they do is *how they feel* while doing what they enjoy.

How do they feel?
Highly focused.
Deeply gratified.
Connected to a larger purpose
as if something valuable is being developed within them.
Who doesn't want that?

This feeling doesn't come when they are relaxed or taking drugs and alcohol or consuming the "the expensive privileges of wealth." "Rather," he says, this experience involves "risky and difficult activities" that "stretched the person's capacity and involved an element of novelty and discovery."

Ultimately, simple creative organization can help create the conditions for us to be in flow more often. Creative organization can help us enjoy our work and tasks, be gratified by taking regular steps toward big projects, and feel as if we are the agent of what happens in our creative life — that we're **the creative actor** and not the helpless actee.

What to do?

A SOLUTION: Mind Rooms

One tool of creative organization is what I call "Mind Rooms."

Think of rooms in a building. A room shapes physical space. Its demarcation from other rooms suggests its function and what you'll spend your time doing in that room. Traditionally, a house's physical rooms had distinct functions. You cooked in the kitchen, ate in the dining room, lounged in the living room, evacuated in the bathroom, and slept in the bedroom. Of course, functions spill over. Despite what some Feng Shui consultants might advise, we gather and chat in the kitchen. We eat in whatever room is convenient. We nap on the living room sofa. We work in the bedroom.

A Mind Room shapes mental space. It's a tool to help the mind focus on one project at a time, give meaning to multiple small tasks, and keep taking consistent creative action toward completing projects. Ultimately, using Mind Rooms can help you see at a glance where your mind is spending time and where your actions are prioritized or not.

Here are 6 simple steps to begin shaping your Work Flow with meaning, rhythm, and gratification.

1 USE YOUR DOWNLOAD NOTEBOOK

First, just "get it out." Take your pocket notebook and label it "Download Notebook." Use this notebook for two purposes: One, whenever you realize — when somewhere other than in your work space — you need "to do" something. Write down the task in a simple verb-centric imperative: Call Cindy re: the event video or Research for answers on solar energy efficiency or Draft third chapter opening.

Two, observe when you need to download all of the "to-do stuff" that is weighing down your mind. Before you succumb to "Overwhelm," download. Simply list everything you need to take on within the next week, two weeks, or three weeks.

② SEE THE PATTERNS

This list should help you recognize patterns and categories that your mind focuses on for your work and your life. These categories will become the basis for demarcating your Mind Rooms. For instance, my work and life generally fall under these categories: **Deep Creating**, **Client Prep & Meetings**, **Training & Programs**, **Meditation/ Practice/Deep Space**, **Business Development & Operations**, **and Personal (Family, Homesteading, Friends, Errands)**.

For now, those are my six core Mind Room Categories. Granted, one room feeds the other the way my study feeds my client conference room, but they each still have mutually exclusive functions.

One of my client's basic categories are Writer, Professor, Events Coordinator. Another client's categories are [name of big copy writing/marketing client], Other Marketing Clients, her novel. Another client's categories are Enterprising, Creating, and Clients.

WRITE THE NAMES OF YOUR 4-6 MIND ROOMS:

1.

2.

3.

4.

5.

6.

Tip: Keep the name simple, recognizable yet personable.

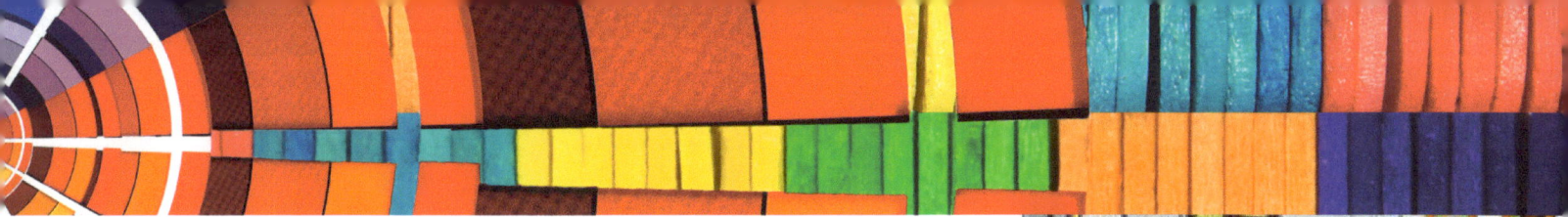

3 PAINT YOUR MIND ROOMS

We paint rooms in our house and office for a reason. We want a room to evoke a mood that matches its function. We want to feel a certain way in that room. Maybe we want to endow the room with our personal signature. A bedroom painted Mediterranean sunset orange evokes a different mood than a red reading room.

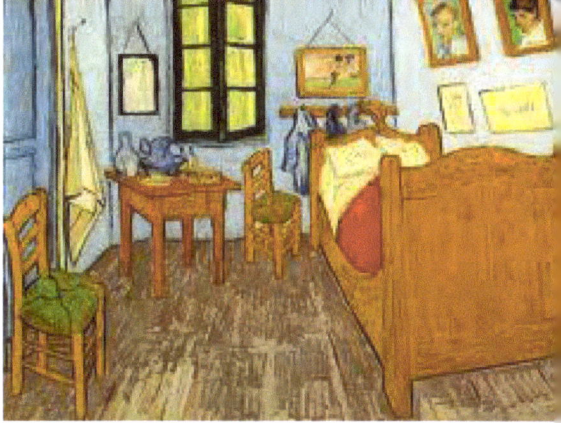

You can see the color of each of my four rooms above under #1. Each of these colors means something to me. My mind also likes some order, and the colors visually help my mind stay ordered (See the white wall photo.) Aesthetics matters to productive, successful creative people. Color-coding our task categories (a flat translation of "Mind Room") can bring small delight and pleasure. Ample evidence points to the fact that positive emotions keep us going.

Behavioral scientist writer **Winifred Gallagher** reviews this research in her highly readable book **RAPT: Attention and the Focused Life** (The Penguin Press, 2009). She notes, "[G]ood feelings such as affection, pride at a promotion, and enthusiasm for a new project are the carrots on the stick that keep you moving smartly along life's up-and-down road." So give each of your Mind Rooms a distinct color. Assign one color of Post-It notes to each Mind Room.

MIND ROOM NAME	COLOR
1.	
2.	
3.	
4.	
5.	
6.	

Rename these rooms to accord them personal meaning. Let's say that you are excited to amp up your client service this year. So, you rename your "Other Clients Room" to "Client Astonishment Room." That simple shift highlights and reminds you of your emotional and personal goal.

Next, from your Download list, transfer one to-do onto an appropriately colored Post-It. So, if you have a Mind Room called the My Novel Room that is painted red, you might write on a red Post-It note a specific task or intentional focus such as, "Sketch character portrait of Andi" or "Draft into Ch. 3 Scene." Keep the language simple and verb-oriented.

This shaped list **reframes** our small tasks into meaningful rooms.

Reframing is an empowering tool to help us creatives stay motivated.

From the work of Positive Psychology psychologists, reframing shifts us from underlined_link_learned helplessness to empowered thinking, feeling, and action. So, instead of seeing "buy envelopes" or "send our client letters" on a list of 38 random to-do items, these tasks now sit in the Client Astonishment Room.

④ BUILD YOUR HOUSE

All you need is a simple white board and/or computer calendar program. Manufacturers make miniature white boards that can stand or hang. You also can buy white board "wall" material as shown in the photographs from my study.

If you like the tactile, physical option — as I do — then draw a weekly or bi-weekly grid on your white board, something simple like this:

SUN	MON	TUES	WEDS	THURS	FRI	SAT

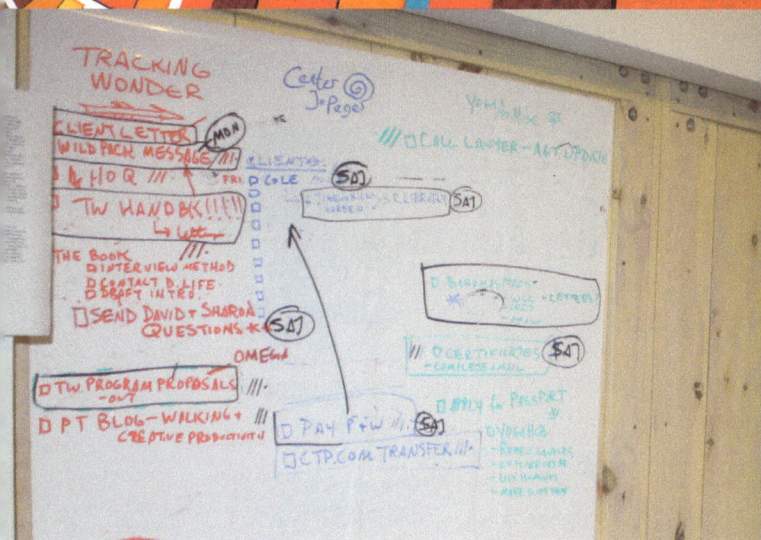

Here is what my Mind Room list used to look like on the dry-erase wall adhered to the back of my study's barn door.

Here's a more updated version using Post-It Notes. At the bottom, I have a place for Post-It items that I recycle and re-use month to month.

I also have a BACKBURNER corner to note big projects and tasks on the horizon.

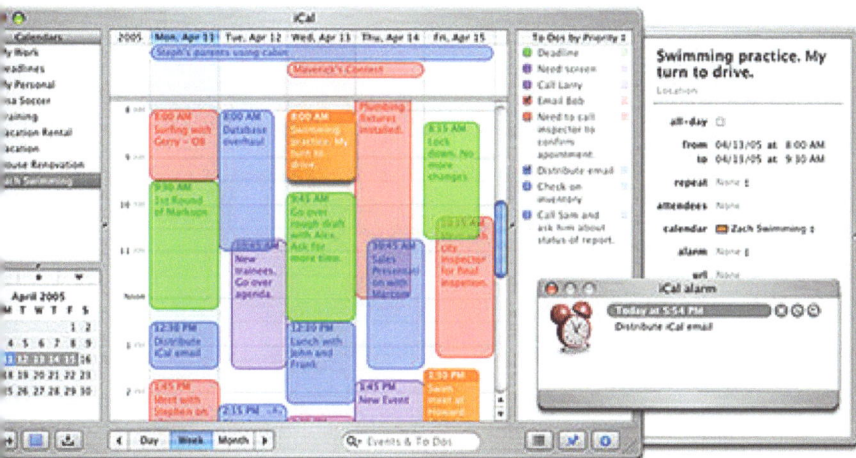

Otherwise, iMac computers come now with a nifty, intuitive **iCal** program that lets you color-code your Mind Rooms and maneuver color-coded tasks around.

For PC computers, **Microsoft Outlook Calendar** offers a comparable calendar program. (Note: One key difference I've found is that iCal lets you divide tasks into 15-minute increments whereas Outlook lets you divide tasks only into 30-minute increments. Sadly, I also find iCal's system of color-coding Reminders requires more steps than Outlook's layout.)

TIP: I play with both the tactile white board Post-It system and the calendar system. The white board helps me play and step away from my desk. The calendar helps me secure and organize my meetings and my days. Once I'm in a day's work flow, I like to click on my calendar and see where my mind is supposed to be. This relieves a great deal of anxiety and increases a great deal of gratification.

5 EVERYONE, TO YOUR ROOMS!

Here's where the pleasure begins. **Place each task within a Mind Room.** That is, take each Post-It note and schedule when you aim to be in that Mind Room for that specific task. Tip: Once a week, maybe on a Sunday afternoon, have a weekly Time-Sculpting ritual. Pour a favorite beverage or gather a delightful snack, and assign your tasks to their painted Mind Rooms and intended time slots for the week.

While creating this list of tasks, you might realize you need to add another Mind Room. Go ahead.

So, rather than having a long, random to-do list to get things done, you will have three to six columns or rooms of action items.

You might create partitions for projects within your Mind Rooms. Within my Writer Mind Room, I have divided space for The Book, Short Stories, Poems, and Blogs. Currently, The Book and Blogs are more occupied than the other two.

This simple step brings flexible order to an overcrowded mind. At a glance, the list also will help you see which room you need to spend more or less time in.

6 BUNDLE & STAY IN ONE ROOM

My experience with myself and my partner projects & clients corroborates the research: Our attention and vitality generally flow in optimal waves of 90 minutes.

When possible, try to "bundle" your tasks within a single Mind Room for 60-90-minute flows. That is, see if you can sequence a series of tasks under your "Create" Room together or a series of tasks under your "Business Operations" (like "Check email" or "Update social media") together for 90-minute periods.

Doing so is essential for minimizing our irrational tendency to fritter away time checking email, hanging out in social media spaces, and reading distracting gossip on news sites.

Really, most of us have to do a lot of work to re-train our minds to "Stay in Your Room — and Enjoy It!" Think of such mind-discipline as parenting your best self. It wants compassionate and vigilant guidance.

Be flexible. Inevitably, plans change. Like, several times a day. One beauty of this system is you can move the Post-Its or the computer calendar items around.

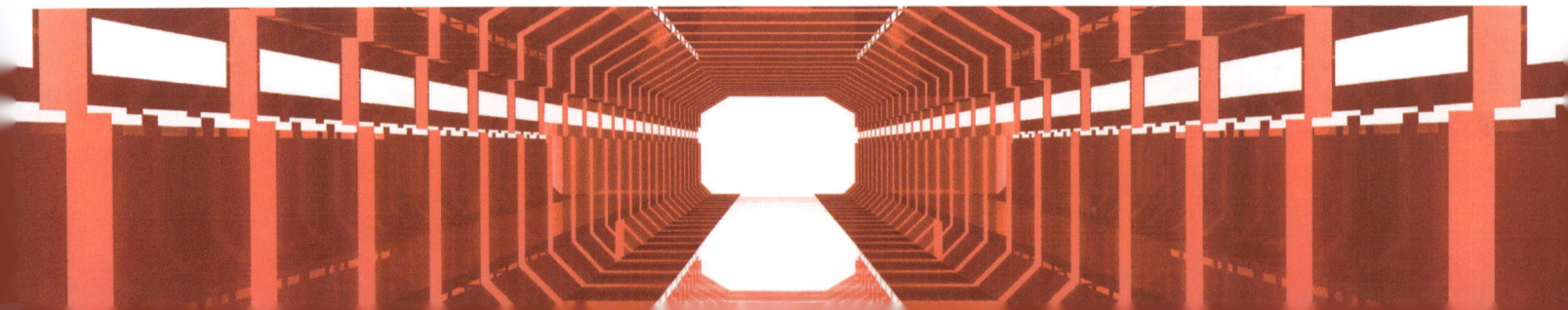

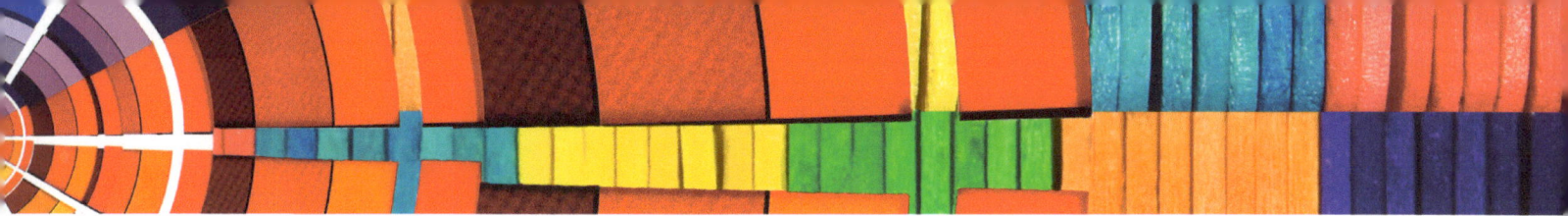

7 THEME YOUR DAYS

You might even get to the point that you can give your mind some regularity to certain days of the week. If you're a coach or consultant, can you designate certain days each week or each two weeks to client meetings? Can you designate certain days to research and big project development and deep creation? Can you designate regular times each month for rejuvenation?

Although mindless routines can squash creativity, mindful routines and regular rhythms give your best self a wide berth in which to roam into the unknown and still know it's safe to do so.

If we enjoy our work — even the small tasks — we're more likely to be more productive and efficient. A small time investment in remodeling your mind might pay off in the long run.

Let me know what you think and what happens.

See you in the woods,

Jeffrey

1. REMEMBER THE DEAD LINE.

In 1944, Miklos Radnoti knew the Nazis would shoot him and the other Jews marching across Hungary any day, any hour. When his wife later had his body exhumed from a mass grave, they would find a notebook of poems tucked in his field jacket's pocket. Somehow, he stealthed out a pen, the sound of gunfire rattling like bones, and wrote a series of poems.

Radnoti's persistence is a haunting reminder of my mortality, of this odyssey's limited time.

The pressure of time, the fact of mortality, the real dead line, compels me to create, and to create with awareness and intention.

2. TANGO WITH TIME.

All of us creatives tango with time. Most creatives cannot wait until their kids go off to college or until retirement or until divorce or until they quit a job to begin their real work. Gratified creatives with packed lives create before the family gets up or in "pockets of time" — on the subway or in the forty-eight minutes between when their children have fallen asleep and before they themselves fall asleep.

One way or another, we'd be wise to make peace with time, stop fighting it, and avoid bemoaning its scarcity. There's plenty of time to be had, it turns out, and if we can't change the way chronological time works, then we can change the way we work with it.

Instead of managing time like some begrudged worker, we can shape it. Think of yourself as a potter more than a manager.

To show up and shape time as a creative has less to do with calendars and more to do with loving the mind. And the body.

Creativity is not about waiting for the muse – despite Elizabeth Gilbert's charming spin on the Greek muse (I've written about the "M" word for Creatives elsewhere).

Creativity is about showing up and shaping time for the muse.

3. TIME CRUNCHER OR TIME STRETCHER?

Feeling gratified in your work doesn't depend solely upon whether you have too little or too much time. Most creatives are Time Crunchers or Time Stretchers.

Time Crunchers have packed lives filled with obligations of family, colleagues, clients – and a variety of inopportune surprises like car failures, employee failures, and broken ankles that plunder the pockets of time they had allotted for their meaningful work.

I'm in this category most of the time. I develop three complementary businesses, manage a small team, write, work with clients, develop client products & events, and guide a group of facilitators – all while I engage my wife and little girl, keep up with friendships and extended family and an aging car and an aging cat and an aging body, and do things for my soul like keep up the homestead and tend to the small orchard out back and keep politically involved.   You know this life, right?

Time Stretchers, by virtue of trust funds or investments or self-employment or retirement or smart & modest living or excess vacation time or retreat time, have enviable hours to shape. And both groups must learn to shape time in order to feel gratified in their work flow. I'm in this category about 2% of the year when I go on extended creative retreats and self-created business immersions.

Unless you factor in the fact that – because I have no boss and commute to the study and conference room at the back of our farmhouse – 90% or more of my time I shape, not someone else.

4. CHANGE YOUR MIND ABOUT – AND WITH – DISCIPLINE.

We have baggage around our experiences of discipline. We're hard on ourselves. We whip ourselves. We cuss ourselves.

As a consequence, some coaches and bloggers advocate dissolving discipline altogether. They come up with euphemisms and ways to say in essence, "You don't need to be disciplined."

The word discipline comes from Latin words related to "teach" and "train" and "follow." A disciple follows one who is worthy of being followed. Here's where we Americans freak out. But in the case of being creative, you're not following a parent or guru. You're letting your Everyday Mind follow Your Best Creative Self. You're letting Your Everyday Mind follow your Mirror Mind.

In The Happiness Hypothesis, social psychologist Jonathan Haidt describes the mind as an elephant in part capable of being trainable but not controllable. The untrained elephant simply isn't as happy as the trained elephant (And anyone who refers to the novel Water for Elephants in response is missing the point!).

Harnessing the mind's attention can be an act of love for the mind. You're tending to it and bringing out its best capabilities.

And you're acknowledging that *you can pursue mastery of your mind's crazy fluctuations.*

5. MIND'S MIRRORS

Time-shaping has a lot to do with the creative mind's mirrors and rooms. Think of Alice in Wonderland. A part of your mind – Everyday Mind – has no mirrors. It only has one-way input streams that it's not even aware of. It receives and reacts to the news being read on the Internet, the messages popping up on the iPhone, the little girl screaming and refusing to put on her shoes. We need a vital Everyday Mind in order to stay creative and optimal.

But when Everyday Mind runs the controls for hours, days, months, years!, then it really becomes Reptile Mind – a primal place of reactivity instead of creativity (a favorite anagram). Raw fight-or-flight mode. Devastating for the creative's long-term motivation and physical energy.

Everyday Mind and its slippery shadow Reptile Mind account for about 5% of the mind's activity at any given moment. That according to George Lakoff and other cognitive scientists.

Another part of your mind has mirrors. In Mirror Mind you can witness Everyday Mind as it's receiving input. It's almost like you're having a simple lucid dream. You can hear Mirror Mind talk to you and say, "Oh! Your computer just froze for the fifth time in a week. Everyday Mind is getting angry. Oh! Your neck is tightening. You stopped breathing."

Apply Mirror Mind to time-shaping: "Oh! You're wanting to watch the opening episode of Homeland instead of working on that design project" or "Oh, look at that! You've spent the past hour tidying up your studio for the fifth time this week or reading the political gossip on The Daily Beast instead of writing that scene for your novel – or dreaming up your next webinar course – or developing that new speaker's series for your agency."

There are three tricks (at least) to using Mirror Mind to your advantage.

One: **Open Mirror Mind at the moment of decision** – at the moment you're typing in the Netflix url or at the moment you're reaching for the dust rag.

Two: **Forget guilt**. Mirror Mind is not interested in self-flagellation. Only reflection the way a still pond lets the sky and willow see themselves.

Three: **Change the mirror into a crystal ball**. At the moment of decision, imagine yourself doing the work you love and doing it in a way you love to do it.

All three of these factors — witnessing the moment, abstaining from self-judgment, and imagining your best self — quiet the reactive amygdala and wake up your brain's frontal lobe. This balance shapes your mind that in turn helps you shape time.

Yeah, but when in the moment, how do you flip out of Reptile Mind that simply wants an 88% dark chocolate bar and an episode of Glenn Close destroying everyone in her wake in Damages? How do you bring out the non-judgmental mirrors?

6. USE MIND ROOMS.

Mind Rooms are designated areas where your mind typically dwells during the day and throughout the week. You can use Mind Rooms to shape your obligations and intentions.

7. SHOW UP FOR YOUR MUSE

45 OR 90 MINUTES AT A TIME.

Once you have your mind rooms shaped, make appointments to show up. Every Sunday evening, I spend 1-2 hours shaping how Monday might flow and the rest of the week. I prioritize Writing Time and Dream Time (what I call those periods of project development, workshop development, client product development, and business development). They get priority. They lead. Because they inform everything else. If they don't get due attention, everything else feels less than astonishing. And, frankly, I expect astonishment every week.

At the 99U Conference last May, I heard Tony Schwartz of The Energy Project speak about sprints. His trademark idea is that we're better off focusing our energy on shorter work periods divided by breaks for replenishment than by trying to work in marathon periods.

You can write a book — at least in part — in 45-minute increments. But only if that 45 minutes is highly focused.

8. BUNDLE YOUR WORK.

Once I have my tasks grouped in my Mind Rooms, I can schedule them accordingly. I bundle client meetings next to each other on the same days. I bundle client preparation tasks on the same days. I bundle email correspondence in 45-minute chunks.

Bundling tasks this way is consistent with what brain science studies repeatedly have shown us about the hazards of multi-tasking. We're not wired well to handle multiple tasks simultaneously if those tasks call upon different parts of the brain.

I use Microsoft Outlook Calendar on my PC laptop and Mac's iCal on my Mac desktop to color-coordinate my Mind Rooms and to bundle tasks.

9. REPEAT THE NO-MATTER WHAT MANTRA.

A client I worked with two years ago wanted to get her business developed to another level of meaning and financial stability. But her oldest of three sons was approaching adolescence, her husband was entering a sort of mid-life conundrum, and her parents weren't faring so well either. But after attending one of my creativity retreats, she returned home ready to create No Matter What. And a son broke his leg in a skiing accident. And her mother got ill. And you know? My client kept creating. She kept her 30-minute and 45-minute appointments with her muse. No Matter What.

10. SHAPE BEGINNINGS, MIDDLES, AND ENDS.

Be aware of your body as you create. Call it "Creative's Pose." That act of awareness makes your actions more intentional and increases your chances of bringing out the mirrors while you create.

Begin: Shut off email alerts. Use Freedom or other cool tools to reduce fret. At the beginning of a sprint, state or write down a focus intention. Just breathe for five cycles. Count in to three or four seconds, and count out to three or four seconds. Why? More frontal lobe stimulation. A simple way to quiet down the Reptile Mine and bring out the mirrors. Set a timer.

Middle: Watch your impulses. Catch your hand taking the cursor to check emails. Focus on the breath again. Observe tension. Talk to your best self in friendly, encouraging ways — even if you're engaged in creatively critical activity like revising a design or assessing a project's next steps.

End: Acknowledge the end of the designated time. Try not to obsess into marathon mode and burn yourself out. Bow out. Feel gratitude for that sprint.

11. BE THELONIOUS MONK: REGULAR, NOT RIGID.

The creative mind loves meaningful repetition.

For several years, I've lead a course for creative and creative writers in the Bahamas that gives creatives hands-on, body-on experience in shaping time and much more. The course's key focus is showing you how to integrate specific yogic tools into your creative process with each tool or sequence aimed toward a specific creative end. You can shift your breathing a certain way to heighten your imagination. Another way to perk up your energy. You can move the body in certain ways to birth fresh insight or focus as you create.

One reason Tracking Wonder tools such as Yoga As Muse work so well with creatives is that a creative mind can memorize its simple patterns, and the simple patterns are pleasurable to the body and brain. It's a type of repetition the creative mind wants more of. It's a type of repetition known to create more brain cells — not a bad thing for flexible thinking.

But with all of the above time-shaping and mind-harnessing activities, I have to watch myself. I resist rigidity. I set my intentions. Shape my calendar. And then flow. If I get "off-schedule" — which I do every day — then that's okay.

If I've created a monastery for my creative self, then the main monk in charge is Thelonious Monk. Now that man was disciplined, and he was a master of his mind and his métier — all so he could improvise in the moment.

12. DO IT FOR THE DAY. AND FOR THE CAT.

Every day stretches wide and long or short or narrow. The hours wave by. Or they march. Or they creep. Or they saunter.

As those hours go by, your muse is waiting. Don't stand it up.

My gray long-haired cat is 15, maybe 16. Two weeks ago, he stopped eating and started hobbling. We thought he had kidney failure. But with a shot of steroids and pain meds, his spine stopped hurting, and he started eating again. This morning he wobbled outdoors to sniff and roll in my wife's browning garden. He's making the most of the day.

It's no coincidence his name is Miklos. After the poet. He's a furry reminder.

FANTASIES OF FREEDOM CAN TRAP CREATIVES & ENTREPRENEURS

Four-hour work weeks, lounging on a beach while "passive income" streams in.

Fluid days of getting lost in canvases and pages, paintings and books in steady demand.

These fantasies sound dreamy, right?

You're pressed for time. You're over-scheduled. You're inundated. You're making snail's progress on projects you care about.

The problem with those structure-less fantasies is that for working entrepreneurs or creatives a toxic resentment creeps in toward obligations to clients or co-workers. Obligations to family. Taking care of the business of life. Prison bars, all of them, that keep them from their fantasy of freedom.

What I say about freedom might irritate you, but here's what I've noticed.

People who've become their own boss — entrepreneurs, freelancers, creatives — fall into one of two categories.

For the over-schedulers, work life bleeds into and drowns the rest of life. The 24/7 online life has no boundaries.

On the other extreme, the anti-schedulers bemoan that days float by with no progress made on what matters.

Newbie entrepreneurs and business artists often make the mistake of tossing out the work schedule altogether.

We rebel against structure. Something in us that wants to defy the "9-5 scheduled life" and say we're our own boss also wants to bust free altogether of "the scheduled life."

But unless we have a patron, benefactor, former corporate job savings, or trust fund, that rebellious frame against schedules and structure ironically could imprison us in a cognitive trap. In fact, even if we have cushy financial resources that free up our time, we still can be trapped.

It turns out that the experience of flow and flourishing does not happen out of conditions of wealth and luxurious relaxation, according to Mihaly Csikszentmihalyi, whose break-through studies in creativity gave us the term "flow."

Instead, flow arises out of meeting challenges of our own volition. And the challenge of time and focus are what I hear most often among the people I work and talk with.

So how do we trip that fantasy trap? Maybe much has to do with how we view freedom and structure.

You might say freedom is "the ability to do what I want when I want." Fair enough.

But that definition often comes with those fantasies of structureless freedom. "Carefree" equals freedom.

But the perception as much as the circumstances create the prison. Irritating, right?

What if our perceived lack of freedom has less to do with our "online 24/7" times?

What if our experience of freedom has everything to do with how we regard our time, direct our mind, and guide our actions each day and week strategically or not, artfully or not?

Flourishing at Google

Consider a recent longitudinal study being conducted at Google. The study examines work place conditions among Googlers and specifically examines how they address their work schedule.

The Segmenters as the researchers call them clearly separate their work life from the rest of their life. They don't take work-related emails home with them. They get good sleep at night.

The other group lets it all bleed. They work crazy hours at night. The "rest of their life" is work.

Segmenters make up 30% of the group. Most of the other 70% wish they could function like Segmenters.

Something to note here: People thrive under different working conditions. To Google's credit, they're seeking how to create different work environments and conditions that facilitate the Segmenters and the non-Segmenters. But they're also sensitive to how their very creations have perpetuated restless workers instead of artful workers.

What if the Artfully Scheduled Life, when shaped strategically, could lead to more fulfillment and a different kind of freedom for some people?

I've witnessed it happen over and over again.

For a young musician. He had no scheduled life and bountiful aspirations. He felt paralyzed by possibilities. But he changed all that and learned how to advance his aspirations artfully.

For a veteran psychologist. She has a brilliant, sensitive mind, but anxiety and obsessiveness paralyzed her. At first, she refused to schedule her life, but an artful approach to scheduling, prioritizing, and pursuing mastery in her writing helped her abate distress and assume more agency of her creative life.

For a lawyer changing her practice. Suddenly isolated at home, she had no external forces to hold her accountable to how she scheduled her days. She, too, felt paralyzed by the newfound free time as she wanted to pursue creating new programs, books, and more. Simple strategies helped her reclaim agency of her mind, actions, and pursuit of mastery.

And for couples I've worked with.

One husband and wife are financially independent of each other although are by no means "wealthy." They have a child and an infant. With no formal business education, they each have bustling businesses that impact thousands of people.

They both savor engaging people directly. That's where they each flourish. So they bundle meetings wisely.

They each also have more ideas than either will ever execute. So they have to discern and prioritize and "kill" a lot of projects.

They also relish spending time with each other, friends, children, their homestead. So they partner in their scheduled lives. They each ask for what they want and need. Monthly in-house retreats. Seasonal retreats. Time away.

Their schedules are full. And they both feel free. More often than not.

No perfection. This is a constant work-in-progress. Everyone creates "art" differently especially when the art in question is a day being shaped.

The key is not to surrender agency nor to default to wishful thinking.

Another Frame of Freedom

Maybe we're trapped by default patterns in how we think, act, create, and speak. After thirty, forty, fifty years, these patterns make up who we think we are and what we think is real.

Freedom might come in being able to recognize the tired patterns of how we think, act, create, and speak. And then trip those cognitive traps.

Freedom might come in being able to prioritize what projects matter most.

To act on them consistently with less stress.

To bypass most overwhelm and shape time instead of letting time spend you by day's end.

Best you can. Without perfection but with deliberate artfulness.

It's that kind of freedom I'm hellbent on helping you finesse for yourself and your teams.

Every human mind is wired to thrive within structure. But not in the same way.

———

I know you're pressed for time. Your body's creaking. Your mind's a labrador of distractibility.

I get it. I've been in all of those places. Several years ago, my concentration vanished. A few years ago, Lyme's Disease debilitated my body and stamina. Thrice.

But when challenges mount, I devise strategies. And I execute project after project now. Our business bustles.

Find freedom to create what matters most.

That kind of freedom is business as unusual. It's business as art, and it's what I am working toward for all of us.

THE ART OF SHAPING INSTEAD OF CURSING TIME

My four-month-old girl gawked at my gesticulating form from across the study.

From her jungle-motif seat, she watched my hands as they whipped hieroglyphs — words and arrows and grids — on my new white board wall adhered to the new sliding barn doors. I was determined to get perspective on what projects I could advance — and *how*.

How was I going to continue being a loving hubbie while also advancing a book, launching teaching programs, designing events, meeting responsibilities to speak and present and write, and — oh yeah — care for this precious creature entrusted to me?

My daughter's life span, curiously, correlates with a period when I learned to shape time in ways that have led to my greatest periods of productivity, creativity, and impact.

My wife oversees her own health care practice and office that includes a team of five and serves over a hundred people a week, and it wasn't as if a lot of meditating and hard work had made our lives easier. My daughter had come into the world only after the flames had cleared.

Fifteen months earlier, a lightning bolt landed on a tree outside my study and fused a faulty electric wire in the attic above my studio and then sent flames through my studio and study. 300 volumes, all my clothes in a built-in closet, 25 years' worth of files, and an altar in ash. Those two rooms eventually would be torn down to the foundation, and the rest of the house gutted to its skeleton due to water and fire damage.

I had assumed a near-lawyerly role during a prolonged battle with the insurance company that would delay renovation for eight months. Twice in this time I contracted chronic Lyme from tick bites that left me fatigued, aching, and a bit delirious, and could've put me down for good.

Fifteen months. Emergency mode. Like operating life on a generator or trying to drive your usual 70 miles an hour in second gear.

With the four-month-old now stowed in the safari seat, my wife and I had been back in our 1850 farmhouse, freshly renovated, for a month after bunkering in a house we rented.

I was ready for a new rhythm. In a bright studio and study, I was determined that autumn to find ways to advance my creative projects, make a difference through my business, and meet my ideal of living each day as awake as possible, papadom and all.

My project of projects started that day with a new strategy for shaping time and guiding attention. I continued a modest daily mindfulness meditation practice and daily morning yoga practice — all of 20-25 minutes to complete. Both practices helped anchor my attention throughout the day and ease the Lyme-related and diet-related aches.

But beyond the practices, how would I focus my frazzled attention throughout the day when I had so many projects to advance? All by myself?

———

Most Americans consider themselves creative and view creativity as important. But very few of them feel they're meeting their creative potential.

That according to one thorough international survey. When asked what was the one thing lacking or most getting in their way to meet their potential, almost all Americans' responses could be traced back to time. Most Americans perceive they lack sufficient time to fulfill their creative potential — or money to gain time. My informal Facebook surveys reiterate this same woe.

My clients and the audiences I speak to express similar frustrations. Their desires and ambitions do not line up with their perceived daily and weekly schedules or with their life lines. Something's gotta give, and in desperation they often assume what has to give is something dramatic like a job or romantic commitment.

We are clearly in an Age of Time-Crunch, perceived and real. On the "real" side, economic strain, emergency stages, and unbidden familial obligations consume our limited minutes and hours. But "how much time" we actually have also has to do with the stamina and attention we can devote to any given task in any given hour, not to mention the emotional quality of that hour.

Riffing on time has become a favorite past time, and it turns out that shaping time, I — and scientists — have found, heightens creativity and incites wonder.

———

The four-month-old pulled a string on a plastic lion head that activated a faux-lion roar with a 24-second jungle tune.

I turned around from the white board wall. My little girl's pudgy face lit up, all smile. My little girl. That I could think those words to myself was itself a little astonishing. "We'll figure this out, right, sweetie?" I said. Maybe she had it pretty much figured out. She pulled the string again.

Meanwhile, on papa's white board wall, grids represented months and then weeks and then days. That day and the ensuing weeks and months and next six years would mark a radical shift in how I could shape time artfully.

For years, my friends who didn't get my innate drive to create and work said, "Wait until you get married." And when I got married, they said, "Wait until you have children."

The next six years would become the most productive of my adult life. My shifts didn't all strike me like lightning all at once (I use that metaphor cautiously now.), but my little girl's life almost mirrors the time frame for my shifts in how I created projects and shaped time differently. What did I do differently?

I learned to prioritize and to accept that I didn't have to work on every project right now, all at once. Time shape.

I learned to let go of projects that might have sounded good but might have just been occupying precious time and space in my creative mind. Time shape.

I stopped hoarding limited funds and started hiring not helpers but collaborators. I viewed the expenses not as expenditures but as investments in my best work to make a difference. I hired an excellent website team to revamp my website and launch my new endeavor. A smart virtual assistant helped me navigate otherwise confounding areas of the digital world. My wife and I became expert weekly and weekend schedulers and quickly found the right assistance with child care. We were not going to raise a child alone, either. Time shape.

Gradually, **I would learn the art of delegation and collaboration. My Do-It-Yourself mentality got replaced with a Do-It-Together mindset.** I learned to communicate and translate my 20-plus years of hard-earned experience to the fields of Story design, messaging, audience engagement, authorship, publishing, and creative productivity. Time shapes.

All of these practices and shifts let me focus attention, energy, and time on what I do best in my creativity and business. Six years later, I have eight exceptional people on my team. Our impact has quadrupled. Time shapes.

And ultimately — whether in a classroom, at the writing desk, in a consulting room, before an auditorium audience, or before a webinar audience — *that* more than anything has driven me. To be awake and make a difference.

———

"Having a child forced me to stop wasting time and dawdling my creative hours."

A friend of mine had told me that several years earlier, before we had a child. I didn't get what he meant then. I get it now.

My daughter, six years old now, is a time-marker. I witness how she grows older almost every day, and if she's growing older that means I am, too. It means I have limited time in this day and on this planet. I want to be awake to as much as possible so I can make meaning, make things, and make a difference for her and for the people I and my amazing team touch.

I still have more projects and books in the pike than I can reasonably manage. But being awake for me begins with acknowledging I don't have to curse time's scarcity. I can sculpt it and make something new of it.

If you can make something new out of existing items, why can't you make time anew out of existing seconds and minutes, of sunrises and sunsets, and of the filaments of attention, intention, and action? That's the question I'm still living.

THE TRUTH ABOUT HAVING TIME TO CREATE

Why don't we create as much as we want? What's the one thing that keeps most Americans from being able to create?

If you look at the results from the research firm StrategyOne, you will get one part of the story. The firm surveyed 5,000 adults — 1,000 each in the United States, Germany, the United Kingdom, France, and Japan — in 2012 about their attitudes and beliefs toward creativity and published the results in the state of create study.

85% of Americans surveyed believe that creativity is key to driving economic growth.

Two-thirds believe that being creative is valuable to society.

75% value their own creativity in resolving personal and professional problems.

But here's where it gets interesting: Only 25% feel they live up to their creative potential.

Why?

You could blame our educational system — certainly an easy target that Sir Ken Robinson, filmmakers, and others have turned into a mission.

You could blame the recession and work environment as many respondents noted that they're being asked to be more productive than creative at work these days.

So, here's a key question: Which of the following are your biggest challenges to being able to create? Please select all that apply.
Self-doubt?
Other Personal Obligations?
Other Work Obligations?
Not Enough Time?
Money?
Your Age?

For the Americans surveyed, self-doubt (27%), other personal obligations (29%), other work obligations (22%), and one's age (13%) ranked fairly low.

That leaves two self-perceived blocks:

Time and Money.

54% of surveyed Americans claimed they didn't have the financial resources to let them create.

52% perceived that lack of time kept them from being able to create.

But when you unpack this question, its potential answers, and the actual responses, much if not all of it comes back to time.

Our perception of time is tied to how we view our obligations. If we think we don't have enough money to create, this means in part that we think we don't have enough money to be freed up from other obligations to afford us the solitude and "off-time" necessary to be "on" creatively.

Here's a related stat: More than the Internet proliferation and addiction, the one factor perceived as decreasing our creativity collectively is decreasing amounts of leisure time.

Which I take to mean not vacationing in Margaritaville. I take this to mean not having dedicated time to reflect, daydream, map out, conceive, incubate, and execute on ideas that

swim around but never get captured in the daily flotsam. I assume this is what is meant by "leisure time" because when people experience creative flow, according to Mihaly Csikszentmikalyi (cheek-SENT-me-HIGH), they do so not because of what recreational wealth or drugs bring them but because of being engaged in activities of sustained focus that bring novelty, discovery, delight, and risk.

Two things to do then:
Change your mind or / and change your circumstances. Or both.

I don't intend to make this complex matter simplistic. But there is simplicity to the equation of time and creativity.

If you cannot change your circumstances immediately, you can change your mind's relationship to and perception of time as well your mind's relationship to current obligations and work.

Not feeling as if you have enough time is also a good incentive to cultivate more awe.

But if you could change your circumstances to help you create more, what would you want?

Again the survey question: Which of the following do you wish you had/had more of our could do/could do more of to be creative?

Time to think creatively — 42%

Training to learn and use creative tools — 38%

An environment where you can think creatively — 32%

Tools to create — 35%

But with these together — time, training, environment, tools — you might be wise about how you invest in workshops or summits or conferences or retreats. Take stock of what you really need now and what you're going to come away with other than only cool experiences — although *meaningful experiences* are essential.

In addition to culling research like this — which is part of my job description — I've also surveyed the people I work with and my readers. Specifically people writing or wanting to write the first or next book.

The Tracking Wonder Pack is pressed for time. But they also want an environment that gives them structured time to create and even to collaborate and get supportive feedback. They're kind of tired of winging it alone or processing their Morning Pages or attending retreats that help them feel good for a few days but don't really equip them to return home to create amidst the laundry piles and client calls.

But they also want substantial field-specific and domain-specific tools to help them move forward. They want concrete tools and methods framed in a way that makes sense for their book project, their publishing goals, and their platform and brand needs.

So, with the need for time and money is a need for know-how + an optimal experimental and learning environment.

Here are what I call **The 6 Core Factors to Create:**

I ~ systems or methods for time sculpted, chosen, and prioritized for the sake of creating what matters

2 ~ tools to focus and imagine and be redirected with compassionate vigilance during that sculpted time

3 ~ methods to incubate with deliberate diversions outside of that sculpted time

4 ~ habits to build stamina to sustain the blood sugar-burning activity that creativity is

5 ~ well-chosen, presented craft-specific and domain-specific tools with feedback during practice (this from seminal research in mastery)

6 ~ optimal environment for guided learning, lateral learning, serendipity, good feelings, and meaningful experiences

There are other key factors, too, such as good systems, structures, and even simple and reliable technology.

That jibes with what I want in life *still.* And it jibes with what I want to create for myself and for you. You?

www.ingramcontent.com/pod-product-compliance
Lightning Source LLC
Chambersburg PA
CBHW040749100426

42735CB00034B/124